I SPY
WITH MY LITTLE EYE...
CONSTRUCTION
SITE

WORK IN
PROGRESS

READY? LET'S BEGIN!

Remember: Just like real I SPY GAME,

letters are not in alphabetical order.

I spy with my little eye something beginning with...

E is for EXCAVATOR

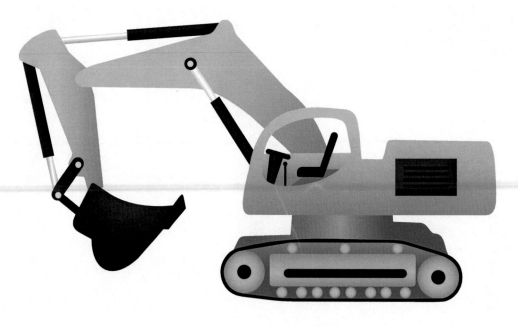

I spy with my little eye something beginning with...

C is for

CRANE

I spy with my little eye something beginning with...

J is for

JACKHAMMER

I spy with my little eye something beginning with...

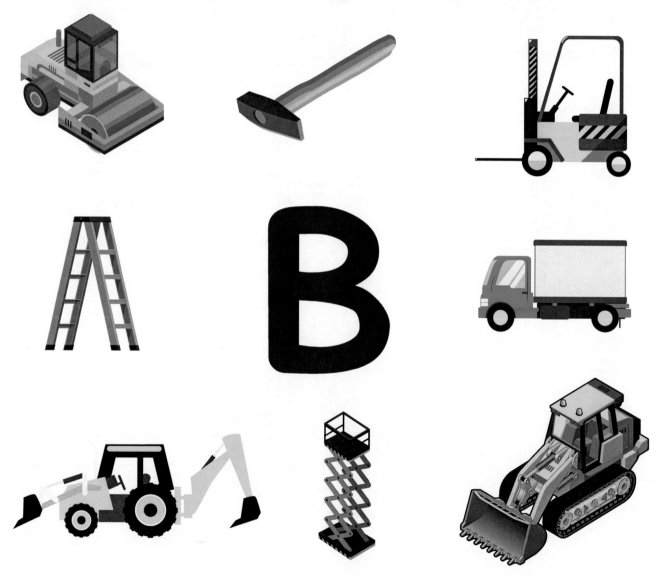

B is for

BULLDOZER

I spy with my little eye something beginning with...

T is for

TRUCK

I spy with my little eye something beginning with...

A is for

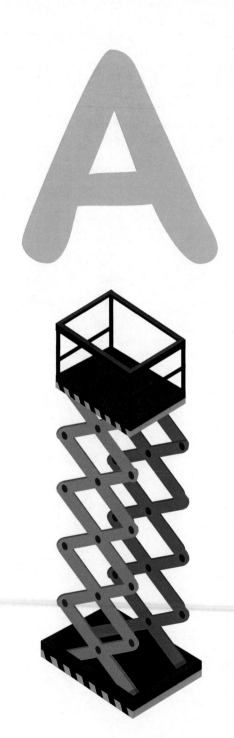

AERIAL LIFT

I spy with my little eye something beginning with...

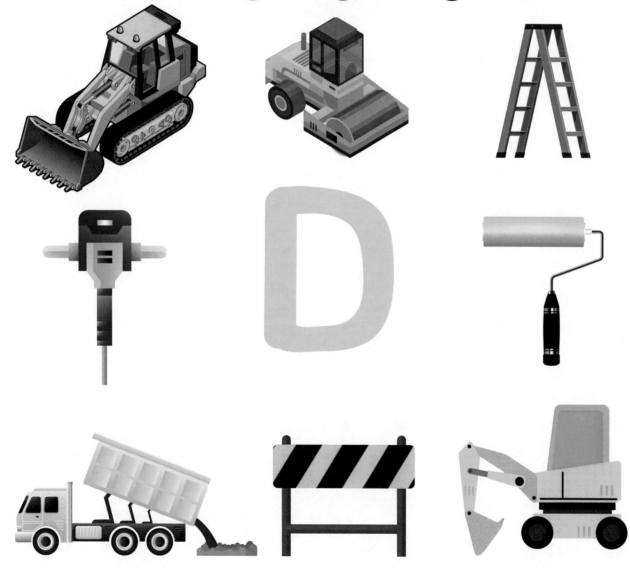

D is for
DUMP TRUCK

I spy with my little eye something beginning with...

F is for

FORK
LIFT

I spy with my little eye something beginning with...

L is for

LADDER

I spy with my little eye something beginning with...

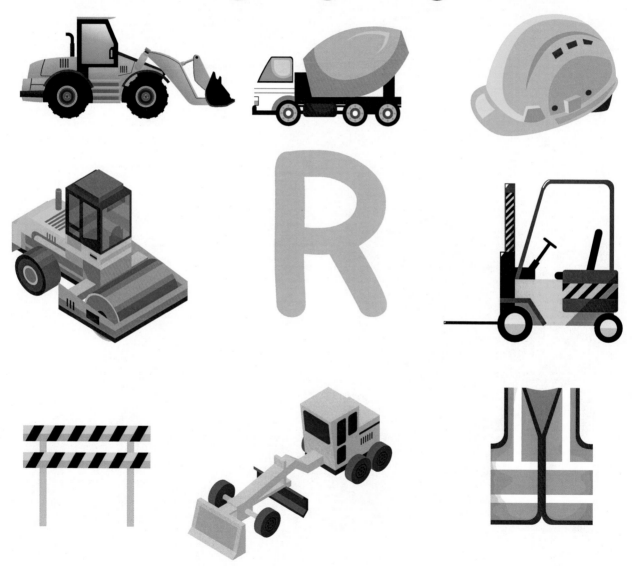

R is for
ROAD ROLLER

I spy with my little eye something beginning with...

W is for
WHEEL LOADER

I spy with my little eye something beginning with...

M is for

MALLET

I spy with my little eye something beginning with...

G is for

GRADER

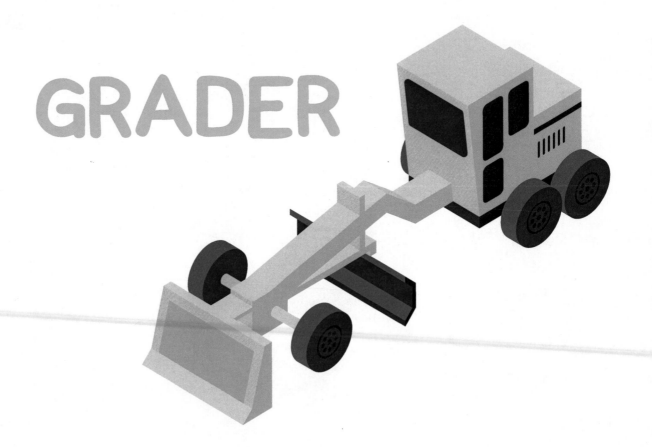

I spy with my little eye something beginning with...

P is for

PAINT ROLLER

Made in United States
North Haven, CT
30 November 2021

11786223R00018